Edge of Conflict

Book 8 of the Junior Jaffray Collection of Missionary Stories

Written by Barbara Hibschman

Illustrated by Elynne Chudnovsky
Cover Design by Step One Design
Portrait by Karl Foster
Based on *Edge of Conflict* by Harry and Miriam Taylor

CHRISTIAN PUBLICATIONS / Camp Hill, Pennsylvania

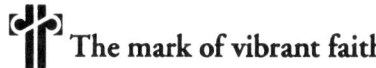The mark of vibrant faith

Christian Publications
Publishing House of The Christian
and Missionary Alliance
3825 Hartzdale Drive, Camp Hill, PA 17011

© 1993 by Christian Publications
All rights reserved
ISBN: 0-87509-514-3
Printed in the United States of America

93 94 95 96 97 5 4 3 2 1

Unless otherwise indicated, Scripture taken from the HOLY BIBLE: NEW INTERNATIONAL VERSION. Copyright © 1973, 1978, 1984 by the International Bible Society. Used by permission of Zondervan Bible Publishers.

Chapter 1

Every Letter Needs a Stamp

Jason and Jessica Hunter enjoyed living next to their new neighbors. Harry and Miriam Taylor were missionaries who had just moved onto their block. It wasn't long until the Hunter family became good friends with the Taylors.

Jason and Jessica called Mr. Taylor "Uncle Harry" and Mrs. Taylor "Aunt Miriam." The Taylors seemed like part of their family and Mother had told them that it wasn't polite for children to call adults by their first names. So, the Taylors became "aunt" and "uncle" to Jason and Jessica.

One day Jessica went to the Taylors' house to return a book Mother had borrowed from Aunt Miriam. As Jessica got ready to say goodbye and return home, Aunt Miriam asked, "Would you put these letters in the mailbox on your way home? I don't think the mailman has come yet."

"No, I don't think he has," replied

Jessica. "I haven't seen him."

Aunt Miriam stopped as she handed Jessica the letters.

"Oh my, here's one without a stamp," she said. "Wait a minute, Jessica, I'll go see if I can find one upstairs."

Jessica waited by the door until Aunt Miriam came back with the stamp. She licked it and stuck it on the envelope.

"There now, that should do it," she said as she handed the envelope to Jessica. "You know, that reminds me of when I was a young girl and I couldn't find a stamp anywhere."

"Did you have to go and buy one?" asked Jessica.

"No, I couldn't go buy one because I didn't have any money. And back then a stamp cost only five cents! You see, I was a student at the Missionary Training Institute in New York and my parents were missionaries in Jerusalem."

"Jerusalem?" said Jessica, looking surprised. "You mean the same Jerusalem where Jesus was?"

"Oh yes, Jessica, I grew up in Jerusalem and when I came back to the United States to go to college I missed my parents so much. I wrote them as often as I could. In those days it took a whole month for my letter to get to Jerusalem and another month for their letter to get back to me. And we never phoned each other."

Jessica was quiet for a moment.

"That's an awfully long time to wait for a letter," she said thoughtfully.

"Yes, it is a long time, but the day I didn't have a stamp God surprised me," continued Aunt Miriam. "I went to the chapel service at my school. The song leader told us to turn to page 12 in the songbook. And there it was!"

"There what was?" Jessica asked.

"The stamp?"

"No, not a stamp—five cents—stuck between the pages. It was all I needed to buy a stamp. It was such a small amount, but God knew I needed a stamp and He wanted to show me He cared even about the little things."

"Wow!" said Jessica. "I always heard in Sunday school that God knows everything."

"Yes, Jessica, He knows and He cares," said Aunt Miriam. "He loves us so much. He just wants us to trust Him for everything we need—even the little things. Now hurry along or you'll miss the mailman."

7

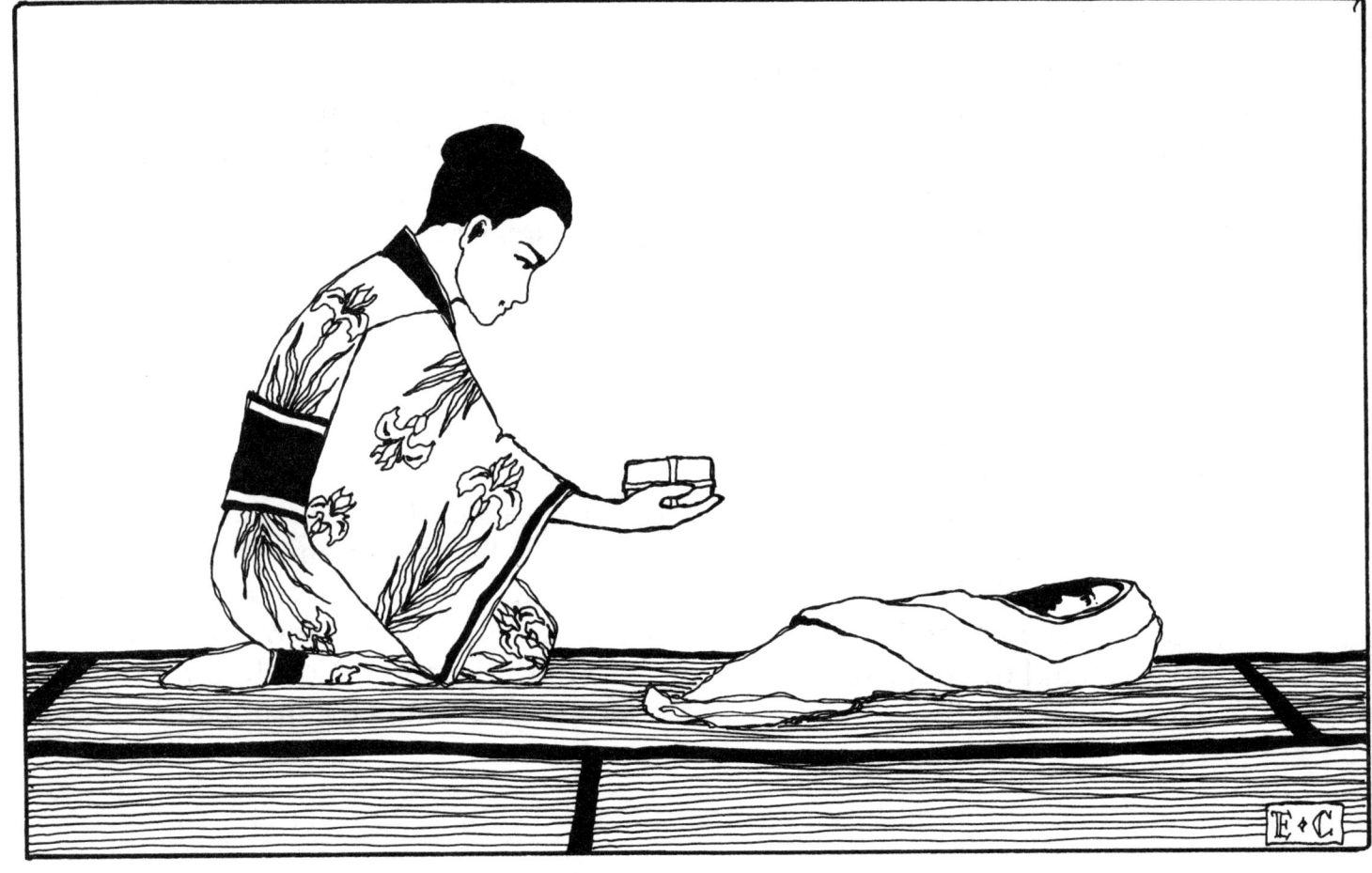

CHAPTER 2

A Baby for Christmas

One evening, during the Christmas holidays, the Hunter family invited Harry and Miriam Taylor to their home. Mother served them decorated Christmas cookies and they drank coffee while Jason and Jessica sipped cups of hot cider.

After a while Jessica excused herself from the table and stood besides Aunt Miriam's chair. When no one else was talking, she asked, "Aunt Miriam, would you like to see the doll I got for Christmas?"

"Oh, I'd love to see it," said Aunt Miriam. They walked into the living room. Aunt Miriam sat on the sofa while Jessica gently picked up a baby doll wrapped in a soft, pink blanket.

"What a beautiful baby!" exclaimed Aunt Miriam.

"She opens and closes her eyes," Jessica explained, "and she wets her diaper when you feed her."

Aunt Miriam laughed.

"Why she's almost like a real

baby! Did you know that God gave us a real baby girl one Christmas morning many years ago?"

"He did? You mean she was born on Jesus' birthday?"

"That's right," answered Aunt Miriam. " Our daughter, Janice, was born on Christmas day. She was the best Christmas present we ever received. She was born in the Philippines right when the war started between Japan and the United States. Uncle Harry and our little son, Don, were taken to prison while baby Janice and I were still in the hospital."

Jessica thought for a moment. She remembered hearing about wars on TV. She knew many people were hurt and some even died in wars.

"Weren't you afraid to live where there was a war?" Jessica asked.

"Yes, at times we were afraid. It was very dangerous," Aunt Miriam replied. "But God kept us safe and gave us food to keep us alive.

"One day when Janice was just four weeks old," Aunt Miriam continued, "I wrapped her in a blanket and laid her on the floor to sleep. There were no beds in the prison camp. A Japanese lady came into the room and noticed the little pink bundle on the floor."

"What did she do?" asked Jessica.

"She bent over and looked at Janice. Then she left the room without saying a word. In a few minutes, she came back with a gift and laid it near her feet. Then she turned and left the room again."

"Was it a rattle or a bib?" Jessica wanted to know.

"Neither," replied Aunt Miriam. "It was a little Japanese *kimono*, a little bathrobe. It was a beautiful gift!"

"Where is Janice now?" asked Jessica.

"Janice is all grown up and married and she has four sons of her own. She and her husband are missionaries just like Uncle Harry and me. You'll never guess where!"

"Where?" asked Jessica.

"See if you can guess," teased Aunt Miriam. "I'll give you a hint. Sometimes, on special occasions, Janice still wears a *kimono*."

"Japan!" Jessica shouted.

"That's right," replied Aunt Miriam. "Janice is a missionary to the people who once held her prisoner. She went to Japan because God's love is in her heart."

11

Chapter 3

Out of Milk

"Hello. Is there anyone home?" called Jason as he rang the bell at the Taylors' door.

Jessica cupped her hands around her eyes and looked through the screen door.

"Aunt Miriam?" she called.

"Why, what a surprise! It's almost dark. Is anything wrong?" asked Mrs. Taylor as she opened the screen door and motioned for Jason and Jessica to come in.

"We're out of milk," answered Jessica.

The children pulled out chairs and sat down at the kitchen table.

"Mom wanted to know if you have an extra cup or two of milk we can borrow for our cereal in the morning," explained Jason. "She's going to the grocery store tomorrow, so she'll pay you back then."

"Oh, I'm sure I have plenty," responded Aunt Miriam as she looked inside the refrigerator. "In fact, here's a quart that hasn't been opened yet. You can have it."

"Yeah!" cheered Jessica, swinging her legs back and forth under her chair.

Aunt Miriam sat down at the table with the children. "I remember once when *our* family was out of milk, too."

"Did you have to borrow some from your neighbors?" asked Jason.

"No," she replied, "our neighbors didn't have any either. It was when we were prisoners during the war. Janice and I were staying in a big house with the other mothers and small children. The prison camp had a few goats and a cow that gave us milk, but they went dry."

"What do you mean 'they went dry?'" asked Jason.

"It means cows can only give milk for a certain period of time and then they run out."

"So, what did you do? Babies and children need lots of milk," said Jason thoughtfully.

"For a while we would grind beans into a fine powder and mixed it with water. We even drank the milk from the big water buffaloes that worked in the fields."

"Yuk!" interrupted Jessica, wrinkling her nose. "That must have tasted awful!"

"Well, it didn't taste so great," Aunt Miriam agreed, "but we knew it was good for us. It wasn't long until the water buffaloes went dry, too. We were desperate—no beans to grind, no cows or goats to milk. Even the water buffaloes were dry. One night we prayed, asking God to provide milk for our children."

"I know what happened," exclaimed Jason. "God made the cows and goats give milk again!"

"Well, God certainly could have done that if He wanted, but He did something even better," replied Aunt Miriam. "When we got up the next morning, there were five new cows standing outside the camp gate! No one knew where they came from, so we let them in. We knew that God had sent the cows there just for us."

"It's just like you and Uncle Harry always say," Jessica noted.

"What do they always say?" wondered Jason.

Aunt Miriam knew. "God will always provide for those who love and obey Him. He hears and answers the prayers of His children."

"I'm glad *we* don't have to milk a cow right now!" chimed in Jason.

Aunt Miriam laughed. "No matter how God meets our needs, it is always good—whether it's out of a refrigerator or from a cow at the gate!"

CHAPTER 1

A Medal for Harry

The North Carolina morning sun beamed through the tall pine trees as Harry Taylor walked briskly toward the Hunters' house. *I know I have a Phillips screwdriver somewhere,* he thought to himself. *Maybe there's a box we didn't unpack.*

Uncle Harry stomped the red clay off his shoes as he stepped up on the Taylors' porch and rang the bell.

"Hi, Uncle Harry," Jason said cheerily.

"Good morning, Jason. Is your dad home?"

"He left about five minutes ago to take Jessica to her piano lesson," responded Jason. "Mom's out back weeding the garden. Come on in."

Uncle Harry followed Jason into the family room and slid into a big, stuffed chair.

"I was wondering if your dad has a Phillips screwdriver I could borrow. It's the kind that has an 'X' on the end of it."

"Yes, he does!" exclaimed Jason.

"And I know where it is. Wait here, Uncle Harry. I'll go get it."

In a few minutes Jason returned from the garage holding the screwdriver in his hand.

"That's it," Uncle Harry said. "I'm surprised you knew what a Phillips screwdriver looks like."

"Aw, that's easy," explained Jason. "I learned about tools when I worked on my carpentry award for Boys' Brigade. Would you like to see the patch I earned?"

"Certainly," agreed Uncle Harry.

Jason reached up on a nearby shelf and pulled down the special award.

"Mom's going to sew it on my blue shirt today," he said as he handed the award to Uncle Harry. "As soon as I learn one more Bible verse I'll be getting another award."

"Which verse is that?" asked Uncle Harry.

"John 8:32," replied Jason. Again, he reached up on the shelf and brought down a piece of paper with the verse on it. He read it out loud: "Then you will know the truth, and the truth will set you free."

"That's a great verse. Keep working on it," encouraged Uncle Harry. "I never belonged to Boys'

Brigade, but I once got a medal, too—from the King of Cambodia."

"The King of Cambodia?" Jason exclaimed. He couldn't imagine what it would be like to get an award from a king! "What did you have to do to get it?"

Uncle Harry leaned back in this chair as if he knew he would be there for a while.

"Well, I never thought about earning an award from the king. I just did the work God wanted me to do. We were given permission to have a church service once a week in a jail."

Jason moved a bit closer to Uncle Harry. He had never been inside a jail, but the whole idea sounded kind of scary.

"Were you afraid, Uncle Harry?" Jason asked.

"No, not really. Aunt Miriam played her pump organ and I played my trombone as the prisoners marched by us to the chairs in the big meeting room. They loved the happy music and sang along with us."

"Uncle Harry," Jason interrupted, "you said the prisoners sang. Wouldn't it be hard to sing and be happy if you knew you did something so bad that you were put in jail?"

"Yes," replied Uncle Harry. "But anyone—even a prisoner—can ask the Lord to forgive his sins and invite Jesus to come into his or her heart. So even though he still has to stay in prison, he is free in his heart."

"That's just like the Bible verse I'm trying to learn," said Jason.

"You're right. 'The truth sets you free,'" agreed Uncle Harry. "We went to the prison week after week and each time we told the wonderful news of salvation and gave out New Testaments."

"So how did you get the medal?" asked Jason.

"Well, the King of Cambodia came to visit our town and just about everyone went to hear his speech. I was very surprised to hear my name called as the King read the list of those who would receive medals. The king appreciated our work with the prisoners.

"Well, I'd better go and get some work done," said Uncle Harry as he walked toward the door. "Tell your dad I'll return the screwdriver later today. And, Jason," Uncle Harry continued thoughtfully, "the greatest award we can ever receive is to meet someone in heaven that heard about Jesus from us.

"One day I hope to meet some of those Cambodian prisoners in heaven."

CHAPTER 5

A Birthday Party for a Princess

"Aunt Miriam, I want to show you something." Jessica scooted over on the sofa so they could both look at the big cookbook. Jason sat on the other side of Aunt Miriam.

"My, what beautiful cakes! Just look at them!" Aunt Miriam exclaimed as she flipped through the pages.

"Sunday is Mommy's birthday," Jason said. "We want to make her a birthday cake, but we've never baked a cake before. Would you help us?"

Aunt Miriam didn't need to think long about that.

"Of course I'll help you," she replied. "What kind of cake would you like to make?"

"Chocolate," Jason and Jessica said at the same time.

"And what kind of frosting would you like?" asked Aunt Miriam.

"White frosting," Jason answered.

"Well, that will be easy enough," said Aunt Miriam. "I'll call your

23

Mom and see if you can come to our house on Saturday afternoon. I won't tell her that we're going to make a cake."

Jason loved the plan. "Mom won't suspect anything. She knows we love to come to your house."

"Then it's settled," said Aunt Miriam. "I'll pick up a cake mix and some powdered sugar for the frosting tomorrow at the grocery store."

"But we'll pay for it," added Jessica. "We've been saving our allowances for a long time."

Aunt Miriam nodded in agreement.

"That will be fine. Now be sure and keep your secret when you get home."

Jason and Jessica ran down the driveway, chattering all the way home about their special surprise.

When Saturday finally arrived everyone helped with the cake. Jason ran the mixer. Jessica greased the pans. Aunt Miriam measured the oil and water and put the eggs in the batter.

In no time the cake was ready to be put into the oven. Jason and Jessica licked the spatula and the mixing bowl. It was great fun!

Aunt Miriam put everything away and soon the kitchen smelled like chocolate.

Jessica sniffed the air.

"It smells so good in here. I guess you've made lots of birthday cakes, Aunt Miriam," she said.

"Oh, I've made quite a few down through the years, but I particularly remember a very special one made by our daughter, Judy, for a princess. When we lived in Cambodia we invited Princess Rasmey, the King's sister, to our home for a birthday dinner in her honor."

"A *real* princess?" asked Jason.

"Yes, Jason, a real princess. You should have seen her when she arrived in her black limousine. She looked so pretty in her silk wrap-around skirt and matching shawl."

Jason and Jessica tried to imagine how beautiful she must have looked.

"We served the meal on our best dishes," Aunt Miriam continued, "and tried to remember all our manners."

"What kind of birthday cake did Judy make for Princess Rasmey?" asked Jessica.

"Oh, it was a masterpiece! It had three layers and Judy decorated it with white frosting and red cherries. When she brought the cake to the table, Princess Rasmey was so happy and surprised she almost cried. She thanked us over and over again. It was the first birthday cake she had ever had."

"That's how we want Mommy to feel," interrupted Jessica.

"Can we put red cherries on our cake, too?" Jessica asked.

"That's a great idea, Jessica," said Aunt Miriam. "Red cherries for Princess Mom!"

Chapter 6

Sami, the Servant

One day after school Jessica and Jason stopped by the Taylors' house. They found Uncle Harry and Aunt Miriam sitting at the kitchen table. The mail had just come and they were reading a letter with a strange looking stamp on it. It was from Lebanon.

Uncle Harry tore the stamp off the envelope and gave it to Jason for his collection. Aunt Miriam poured two glasses of milk, put some homemade chocolate chip cookies on a plate and set them on the table in front of Jason and Jessica.

"Who are they?" Jessica asked as she pointed to a picture of a smiling man and woman on the table.

"They are Sami and Joy Dagher," said Aunt Miriam as she picked up the prayer card. "They're our best friends in Lebanon. They helped us with our missionary work there."

"Sami is now a pastor in Beirut," Uncle Harry added. "Beirut is a very dangerous place to live, especially if you are a Christian."

"What kind of danger, Uncle

Harry?" Jason asked.

"Well, Jason, there has been a war going on for many years in Beirut. Shootings, bombings and fires. There are lots of homeless people. They are often hungry and need clothes. Sami was even kidnapped!"

"Kidnapped!" exclaimed Jessica. "I would have been so afraid. Was he hurt?"

"No," answered Uncle Harry. "God didn't allow Sami to get hurt even though one of the kidnappers had a gun. And yes, Sami was scared. He was so afraid that he couldn't even pray.

"When the men asked him what kind of work he did Sami said, 'I am a servant of the Lord Jesus Christ.' He told them, 'All I want to do is serve the Lord.' "

Jason and Jessica had heard about kidnappers on TV and their parents had warned them not to talk to strangers.

Finally Jason asked, "Well, then, how did Sami escape?"

"A strange thing happened," replied Uncle Harry. "The kidnappers locked Sami in a room. He thought about how he would probably be killed and how his family and church would miss him.

"About an hour later, the door

opened. A man came in and took Sami to the door of the building. 'We're letting you go,' " he said.

"You mean they just let Sami go like that?" Jason was surprised.

"Yes, that's right," answered Aunt Miriam who had been listening to the story, too. "Sami was so thankful to be free. He knew someone was praying for him. God answered those prayers and Sami is alive today because God hears and answers prayer."

"Later," continued Uncle Harry, "he went back to that same place out in the desert and found the two men who kidnapped him. He told them about Jesus and, before he left, he gave each of them a Bible."

"Wow!" exclaimed Jason. "He is very brave. I wouldn't want to ever see those men again."

"Me either," echoed Jessica.

"Sami went back because he wants everyone in Lebanon to hear the good news of the Lord Jesus," Uncle Harry explained. "Being a servant of the Lord isn't always easy, you know, but Sami doesn't mind taking risks because he is happy telling others about Jesus."

"What do you mean by taking risks?" Jason asked. He wasn't sure he knew what a risk was.

"Well, taking risks means doing things that may be dangerous. Sometimes, because of the gunfire, it can be dangerous to cross a street in Beirut," Uncle Harry replied.

Aunt Miriam continued.

"We pray for Sami and Joy every day. We ask God to keep them safe. We pray that they will have enough money for all their needs. We pray that many people in Lebanon will come to know Jesus as their Savior."

Uncle Harry opened his Bible to the back cover and took out two pictures of Sami and Joy Dagher, just like the one on the table. He handed one to each of the children.

"You can be partners with Sami, the servant in Lebanon, too."

"We can?" exclaimed Jessica. "How can we do that?"

"By praying for Sami and Joy," responded Aunt Miriam. "The picture will help you to remember to pray for them."

"You two better run along now or your mother will be looking for you," Uncle Harry chimed in. "We wouldn't want her to think that someone kidnapped you!"

As Jason put his hand on the doorknob, he turned around, tipped his baseball cap, and said, "See you later, partners."

THE JUNIOR JAFFRAY
COLLECTION OF MISSIONARY STORIES
For additional copies of *Edge of Conflict* or information about
other titles in the **Junior Jaffray Collection of Missionary Stories**,
contact your local Christian bookstore or call Christian Publications
toll-free at 1-800-233-4443.

*Titles coincide with the adult biography series, **The Jaffray Collection of Missionary Portraits**.